MANOJ HAPPINESS

Born in Mannarkkad, Palakkad district, as the son of Idoor Krishnankutty and Indhira Krishnankutty. Currently, holds the position of Managing Director at Manoj and Associates Chartered Accountants in Dubai.

Has worked in various management roles whithin corporate companies for over the past 20 years. Developed expertise in yoga, natural living, and motivational training from a young age itself. Dedicated student of the globally renowned spiritual leader and guru, Sree Sree Ravi Shankar, and also recognized an international practitioner.

Published works : 'Snehikkoo Chirikkoo Santhoshikkkoo', 'Aacharalokathe Ariyan, Chilanka Ninakkay (Novel).

Wife : Shyma Manoj,
Children : Abhirami, Anagha.
Brother : Binoj Krishnan.
PH : 00971526999364, 0547329181
Email : manoj@manojcpa.com, manubgy@gmail.com

English Language
Goodbye to Stress
(Motivation)
by
Manoj Happiness
Translated by
Vijaya Unnikrishnan

Published in October 2023
by Decan Imprint Publishing Co.
Reg. Off: Sharjah Publishing City
Free Zone Sharjah, UAE.
Phone: 00971-551830334
Email : decanimprint@gmail.com

Cover Design : Dwijith

Printed at
Manipal Technologies Ltd.

02/23-24/Sl.No.02/100/NS 18.6
ISBN 978-93-5973-868-0

GOODBYE TO STRESS

Manoj Happiness

DECANIMPRINT

Index

AUTHORITY

The claim which an individual has over another individual, or individuals or society becomes authority. When two people meet each other, they have no authority over each other,but that changes over time. Which is why a king who has not seen his subjects, or the subjects who have not seen their king, are bound or attached to each other by a kind of unseen purpose. In a democracy, it is the people who have the supreme power, the last word. And yet, individually, every voter has to elect a leader whom he does not know personally, and who does not know his likes or dislikes.

The relationship between the king and his subjects,and between the king's representatives and the voter is purely technical. In the ordinary context,it is purely imaginary.In a practical kind of way this seems right. This opposition can be seen in matters of governance. Al though technically it is of the people, by the people,for the people, here the ruling ends up as being for only a small percentage of people.

An individual's life, although he may be independent, is determined by the limitations of his authority. Here he has to take care of his own needs and desires. The independence of the individual is the foundation of his authority.

Self realization is the condition when you come to think of the realization of your own soul. That is why it is said that life is a show of of one's authority. The best way of showing authority is to turn it into service. It is said that those in authority are service minded towards the public.

Napolean Bonaparte said that just as as an artlover loves the arts, and a musician loves his music, he loved hos authority. The arts and music are for the people to enjoy. Similarly governance must also be something that people appreciate and enjoy.

A position of authority is something that is most coveted by anyone.There are people going for that position of authority for their own selfish interests. They must understand that those who wish to be considered mighty, do not know the meaning of true greatness. Authority is never permanent.

Authority is compared to liquor.It goes to the head of the best of people. Too much of it will make the person concerned a slave of own his mind.Such people are the ones trying to control criminals and other similar people. Total authority spoils mankind is a well known saying.

It becomes a dangerous situation when one who cannot control himself, tries to control others. In order to establish authority,and acquire more gold and wealth,is what has lead leaders to war.

The authority of lawmakers must be honoured like the word or law of God.No person who governs, and is in authority, can please every single person according to their individual likes and dislikes. So those who rule,must make it their primary duty to find a way to try and please all. This is what all good governments should do.

Stability and availability of essential commodities are what the people expect fro those who govern. Expansion of the country helps to improve the condition of the lifestyle of its people. The famed novelist Victor Hugo had once remarked that by seeing the women and children of a country ,he could make out their culture and upbringing ,and thus of the governance of that country.

In general, not all ordinary people are looking for a position of some kind in society. Many feel authority is burden on them. So they stay away. If the authorities speak against truth and justice,and make any decisions to that effect, the general public must take a stand and act against them. The strength of those people who do not wish for any position of authority, will go against those who govern, and they will become very powerful. Under such circumstances, the general public must not be allowed to accuse them of whatever they may have seen and heard about their wrong doings. Remeber the path of ahimsa or non violence that Gandhiji took during the fight for independence.

Fire and authority are similar.If you go too close ,you will get burnt. If you move far away it is of no use.A truthful and just person in authority is only imaginary.

BEYOND THE FIVE SENSES

It is a great, wide, beautiful, wonderful, world. Still bigger is the universe that is home to countless number of stars. The known and the unkown in the cosmos is the Supreme. The Supreme is beyond our imagination.

Man is only a creature of this universe. The elephant on earth and the blue whale in the ocean are mightier than feeble man. However, because of the five senseorgans he has, man is able to know the Supreme. He can use his eyes to see, nose to smell, ears to listen, tongue to taste and skin to touch and feel. But he has limitations .His vision is not as sharp as the eagle, nor are his ears as large and sharp as those of an elephant. His sense of smell cannot surpass that of a dog that sniffs his way back. And yet because he is in possession of these five sense s, he is able to lead a better life then other creatures.

Man has the mental capacity to remember what he has seen, the music he has heard, the touch he has felt, the scents he has whiffed, the tastes on his tongue. He can describe and share all this in the form of language and script which he has devised.

There is a vast difference between the world of man and that of other living beings. Even though man cannot be different from nature's ways in birth ,growth and death, the growth period of mankind, when compared to that of other living beings, is highly complicated and diverse.

Every thing that man knows in this world, is through the five sense organs. Because of this, the eyes, nose, ears, skin and tongue are called the knowledge senses. Of these, four sense organs are to be found in the head. Even though there is skin on the face, it is part of the all over skin on the body.

The mind is the cellar or storehouse where knowledge is stored.

Where is the mind situated and what is its form? Investigations are still going on in this field in various ways. The nerves connect the five senses to the brain, making it a storehouse of knowledge. Man has no doubt all the blessings of God, whom He has endowed with such precise knowledge. And yet ,man sometimes is enslaved by the devil. And quite unexpectedly turns into the devil himself.

Why does this happen? The five sense organs take command of man, and instead of bringing out the good in him, the bad pushes its way forth. Profits or feel good factors are achieved only temporarily. I, me, myself. Such selfish thoughts take over everything else.

If you can separate the good from the bad provided by the five sense organs, if you can bring yourself to know the good from the bad, and keep it in the safe haven of your mind, then you can achieve a state of virtue. Your five senses must be trained to do this. Hear no evil, speak no evil and the same with the other senses too.

FOOD FOR THOUGHT

The primary requirement of all living creatures is food. Nourishment required for the growth and development of cells is received from food. The excretion of waste matter from this food taken in is equally important. Whatever is not required for the body is pushed out, whether as solid waste or liquid waste. This is also an indication of one's good health.

"Eat to live, not live to eat" so goes the saying. A person who who has too much to eat will soon have health problems, the main reason being that there will be an imbalance between organs of digestion and those of excretion. So that is why health experts recommend that after a meal, one must still have a small hunger pang!

Dissatisfaction is a major ailment of mankind. No matter how much one has, or one gets, there is no feeling of enough but greedily wants more and more. However the only thing man says enough to, is food. However tasty or not tasty a meal maybe, one has to put a stop to eating, as there will be no room in the stomach! The stomach does not allow storage of more than what is necessary! The stomach cannot go beyond its capacity!

The procurement of food is one of life's fundamental problems. The rich can eat whatever they want. The poorer people, who cannot afford it, eat If and when they get something, or in the worst scenario go hungry. If you look around at the food produced all over the world, you will be surprised at the different kinds of food produced, and the varied food habits of people around the world. Diversity in food production is the result of climatic conditions, and also soil make up.

Cooking today is both an art and a science. Over the passage of time, changes came about in the eating habits of man. Agricultural revolution caused an upheaval in the life of man. Here starts the history of property ownership, of family inherited and personal property. The face of agriculture also changed with the production of machines and modern implements .

A man is what he eats .His character can be determined by his food habits. This has led to to some foods being given heritage status even, in order to preserve its cultural identity. Doctors who practice nature cure,say that it is the food that we eat is our medication.

Food is often considered a mark of obligation. One is expected to sing the praises of and always be grateful to anyone who has given you a meal. A Malayalam saying is that one must show gratitude to whoever has fed you, to the hands that have given you a meal.

Although we can go on and on talking about food, one cannot talk too much about hunger. Hunger enters through a door, causing affection to go out of the window. Love and friendships and such like lasts only as long as there is no place for hunger. Hunger is the main cause for agitation. Let us hope and pray God will present himself in the form of a meal to all who are hungry.

a little hungry.

GOODBYE TO STRESS

The mind and body are always at work .Even if you think you are resting ,and are sitting still doing nothing, we are active. We all know our dreams are the result of our actions. In the body ,breath is doing its job.

There are multifarious activities going on in our bodies constantly. Breathing in and breathing out, taking in colour , listening to sounds, causing feelings like hunger, nausea, acts of blinking, yawning, causing swelling ,all these functions are carried on in our bodies silently and independently.

These actions are carried within our bodies without any pressure. However, with pressure from outside, the regular rhythm of these functions tend to go astray, and cause physical and mental stress. Nowadays there are many ways of controlling such stress.

Everyone has his or her own place in this world. The desire to keep this safe, the burden of the thought that you are responsible for your own self, or for some reason you are unable to complete the responsibilities you have undertaken, these cause undue stress for many people. Anxious and worrisome thoughts go hand in hand and tend to cause troublesome issues.

The thought that you will always be a winner, and all victories will always be yours has to be abolished from your mind first. Of course you must have the confidence that you will be successful in your venture. However, along with it, you must also have a realization of defeat, and be aware of ways to overcome it. This realization must be part of your self confidence. This will enable you to to turn any defeat into victory. You must also try to understand that you are not the only person facing defeat or unable to solve matters. You are only one among millions of such people. You must have the attitude that you are not the only person facing common and everyday problems.

Sleeplesness, bursting into anger, raising your blood pressure, there are many issues like this. If a small smile will solve these issues, you must be prepared to to see it, and smile at yourself.

The old saying of eight hours of work, eight hours of enjoyment ,and eight hours of sleep has disappeared with the passage of time. Even so, there is no change in the basics. Whatever the work, there must be a time for relaxation and pleasure and a time for sleep set aside.

Small health disorders are the result 'of working non stop with no break or rest. If you ignore it, it will lead to greater problems. Such pressure if not recognized, will weaken your health. Mental issues can be recognized by your facial expressions. Say good bye to stress and pressure with whatever is considered necessary for good health like food, water, sleep along with relaxation and pleasure filled moments. You can do it.

IDEAS ARE WELCOME GUEST

A person who arrives in your home unexpectedly is your guest. He maybe someone from another place, sometimes even someone totally unknown, who comes as the sun sets. A guest does not stay in one place, but is always on the move. He does not stay very long, but stops by for a while.

Ideas that come to your mind must be treated like guests, and you must always be prepared to welcome more and new guests. The most important characteristic of new ideas or notions when we welcome them, is that they are never destroyed, they remain either in a person's mind, or in the society.

If the guest is an interesting person, the host learns a lot from his experiences. As a travel ler, he has been to different countries, and met up with various people. This would have influenced him in many ways. His personality may have grown, and he may be the richer for his experiences. It is the duty of a guest to share his experiences with his new host. Every guest's knowledge and new information changes hands. What he distributes may take the form of new ideas.

Travellers and merchants who go about in caravans, we can say are the ones who have raised the cultural level of mankind to this extent, by their talks and sharing of their thoughts and experiences. They are those who have laid the foundation stone for the new world.

New and fresh ideas are generally considered the right of mankind and the world. According to requirement, new inventions come up. New ideas are generated by great souls who live among men, and carve out and make new ways for society.

Ideas are strenghth. Often they show no consideration, and can even be dangerous. Sometimes, like the atom bomb, ideas can turn the world around. Those who are pure of mind, and have the power to work are those in whose minds new notions first burst forth. Religious speakers and those who set up religions, put forward their ideas and thoughts that arise in their minds, which they preached to the public at large.

Just as a guest can change into the host, fresh ideas enter from elsewhere, and establish themselves in society. When it becomes irrelevant, the establishment or institution will then try its level best to get back to its original state.

Those ideas that stick to age old traditions tend to move away from their aim and path. Religion and politics, and other popular institutions, when they move away from their original goals, find fresh ideas creeping into their places.

A person who has only one single thought becomes unnaturally possessed by it. Which is why modern youth must welcome new and fresh thoughts and ideas like honoured guests. Any wrong notions must be kept away.

INDIVIDUALITY, WHAT IT MEANS

The personality of each and every person gives him an individuality of his own.. His looks, behaviour, conduct, speech ,religious practices, likes and dislikes, his sensibilities and thoughts about varied topics and even his way of dressing all lend to his individuality.

Good looks are a trait of some sections of people. There are people of all sizes and shapes all the world over. There are short people, tall and well built black people in Africa, those of Aryan origins in Europe, and also in India, the Dravidian people, the Chinese who have Mongoloid features, all look different and cannot be compared to each other.

Not only by way of looks, but also in complexion people are different. There are whole sections on beauty by Indian poets. Physical features define looks differently in different countries. In India, wide lotus like eyes are a sign of beauty, whereas in China a woman's beauty is judged by how tiny her feet are. Over time, these concepts are changing.

When we talk of beauty related ideas of individuals, we must take into account the health conditions too. Good health, the complexion that runs in families, facial expressions, suitability of organs, these are what make up the form of an individual.

It is not a beauty contest that decides the personality of a person. It is only a way of attracting people.

The mode of dressing is an advertisement of an individual. Sometimes, that which is in the name of fashion, in order to attract others, does not come up to expectations. A particular dress, or material or jewellery or other accessories, or the value of all these, do not raise the status of an individual.

Dress, hairstyle, beard and moustache, use of cosmetics,

handkerchiefs, bags, things in the bag jewellery, watch, hairpins, buttons, gold teeth implants will all become objects of assessment of an individual. No one can complain, or pass positive or negative comments. However, at first glance, the appearance and the way it does not suit the person, is the impression whether a friend or relative or anyone else gets. First impression is the best impression as we know.

A very close friend or relative may gently make a remark and give an opinion, maybe even a small piece of advice. But not beyond. However, someone who has had a fallout with the person concerned ,and has kept it hidden in his head, may make some adverse and scathing remarks.They are the kind of people who like to find fault, and revel in it.

Such fault finding people can be ignored. But it is their accusation that becomes a cause for the individual to wonder about it. Although at first glance there may seem to be no fault, on viewing it a second time, a doubt may arise in the mind of the individual ,causing negative feelings.

Form is to be considered the most important factor of a person's individuality. We also have to take into consideration how one's form undergoes changes over a period of time. They will be laughed at and made fun of, and said to be foolish, if they do not dress according to climatic conditions and if they dress in clothes which are unsuitable for them. Beard, moustache, certain types of head gear, are part of the dress code of certain individuals, which may not be acceptable in other places, and those where climatic conditions are different. This will be taken into account where appearance is considered important.

The individuality of a person also lies in the way he dresses according to the period, the climatic conditions of the place, and change of seasons in the place he lives in. We expect that he will dress according to the present style of dressing and be mature enough to mingle with the society that is present there at that time. Some new fashions are acceptable too. But he must not continue to live stubbornly in the past, without changing his ways.

If an individual's appearance, and way of dressing is according to the times, then it is acceptable. It is a good thing for him if hecontinues to dress well, in a neat and pleasing fashion, as he has been doing all along.

Human nature is not one that can be defined in any particular way. The experiences of a person, joys and sorrows, likes and dislikes, relationships with others during that time, wishes, dreams, there are many such things that happen.

All the world is a stage. Life is a drama. The individual is the actor. He may be the hero, the villain, the clown, the helper, taking on many roles to live his life. Life is the truth, whereas acting is something not his own self. Life is a mixture of tears and laughter. There can be sweetness, as well as bitterness.

Whatever it maybe, it is possible for the mind to make life's experiences always sweet. The first thing to do is to compare another person's difficulties with your own easier and happier experiences. Then you will realize how small your own problems are. You must see to it that you are able to stay away from dangerous situations, and be able to save yourself from trouble.

A firm belief in Sanatana Dharma will cleanse your behavior and attitudes. Speaking the truth, practicing non violence, being sympathetic towards the people you live with, giving alms and donations, keeping up relationships with loved ones, being able to distinguish between right and wrong, all contribute to the making of an agreeable individual. Although it is not possible to always find all these qualities in one person, as far as possible it would be good to try and practice these.

It is your nature, good or bad, that is responsible for how you conduct yourself. I The way you are thinking of what you want for yourself, or what you have to get from someone else, and the way you interact with others, all speak of your conduct.

All living creatures may approach the same given opportunity in different ways, physically, mentally, with or without any aim. Everyone is responsible for their own behaviour. No else has a role in it. When a command is obeyed, for example, "go there", it is the nature of an obedient person to do so. How he goes, is the individual's particular trait or characheristic. He can walk fast, or run, or walk slowly. There may be a reason for this, s ometimes he may not even be aware of it.

Sometimes feelings like anger, doubt, sadness, forgetfulness, joy, worries about dangers, fear of defeat, expectations of victory, and other internal and external reasons all affect general behaviour .This is quite natural.Those who pay particular attention to their behaviour always succeed, and if you can recognize your own faults ,you can improve upon them. A lazy and inattentive attitude will cause failure. This will show in behaviour also.

Understanding the seriousness of a matter shows the individuality of a person. But this does not mean he has to always take every thing seriously and and not enjoy himself. Laughter is a necessity. It is good to laugh ,and make others laugh as and when the occasion arises. You should be able to tackle a serious situation even as you laugh. Otherwise you will be labelled as always serious, one with no knowledge, heartless, arrogant, pretender and such like.

Talking, and lecturing are all ways of putting forth ideas by way of words. Clapping hands makes a sound,which is really meaningless. In the use of words, sound has a specific role to play. So one has to pay particular attention while engaging in conversation.

Conversation becomes an art when it is able to impress the the listener. You must speak distinctly and with claritry of words. There is no need for formal speech always. Then it becomes a subject of ridicule.

Whenever you speak to someone, always make sure you look at their face, and put forth your thoughts clearly. If you speak without looking at the person's face, then the listener will consider it a lack of self confidence. If the person understands the local language, you can use that in a charming way. Try to get your message across without speaking in a long drawn out or round about manner.

When a person has had a part to play in any matter, whether it turned out to be a success or not, he likes to talk about it, and tends to get excited about whatever it is he has done. If it is a matter pertaining to his own prowess, he will brag about it at length! However, if the listener has no particular interest in the matter, he will not like it at all. But if the listener feels it is something that will benefit him personally,he will encourage it!

There are some individuals who have the innate capacity to talk about any subject with great authority. But it is not good idea to show off that quality everywhere,but to know when and to whom to speak to about it. It is better to speak to like minded individuals. And not to people who may not understand and who cannot digest the topic of discussion. Also they may think you are trying to show off or being egoistic. There may be some of your own personal issues, or some things which may hurt another person. If such matters are discussed openly, it does not speak well of an individual.

Scandal mongering, tale telling, being quarrelsome, scolding are all negative qualities in an individual. Often it happens that what starts off as an ordinary conversation between two people, finally ends up in a full blown conflict. This is because of the inability on the part of either person to come to a compromise.

An official meeting is something on a more serious note ,and the way of approach and speaking will be different from everyday street talk. You must adapt the the way of speaking according to the context and place. Then only your individuality will come to the forefront. An interview is a very important event in a person's life. There you must speak and behave with respect. Not knowing an answer, and confessing to it, must indicate the individual's truthfulness. If you are in the company of those who are there to have fun and come to enjoy, in such a place you can engage in light hearted conversation .No one expects seriousness here.

Religious sentiments are everlasting and eternal. A relationship with this is everlasting, so we understand that when talking about this, the person, the situation are taken into account ,and no negative comments are made. This is a permanent opinion. An opinion is an individual's own feelings about an idea. When the policy changes ,the opinion may also change, although the idea will not.

The opinion that an individual has about varied subjects and ideas, depends on his knowledge and wisdom. The relationship the individual has with the subject is what will encourage him to come to a conclusion, not whether he was successful or not. An individual will be successful in his endeavours if he does not have negative thoughts or is not stubborn in his ways. There must be give and take.If there is a problem he cannot really solve at all , backing out of it is not wrong, but also commendable. But it must be in such a way that others concerned must also be made aware of the situation as to why he is withdrawing. Otherwise it will be seen a s running away. Running away is the characteristic of a coward. A coward can never be considered a good individual.

It is a brave new world. It is meant for daring and courageous individuals. Bravery is based not on physical strength, but on mental strength. Keeping in mind the progression and building up of a new world, and working towards making feasible new ideas is a characteristic of a person, reflecting his individuality. Those who are unable to move with the times, and are unable to do justice to the world, and have a negative approach, become the responsibility of society and of good individuals.

Only a person with strong and firm individuality can be the head of a society, or an institution. In other words, only a good individual can become a great leader, or be in responsible positions, or in such a positionwhere he can give out orders. Thus we see how each and every person is an entity by himself.

KINDNESS THE MOTHER OF COMPASSION

Kindness is a very honourable emotion of the mind The mind has many different kinds of feelings and attitudes. A heart full of love has untold number of hands reaching out towards it. The affection that such a person deserves is spread all over.

Where there is no kindness, there is no love. There will be no kind of better or sweet feelings, but there will be anger, injustice, cruelty, and violence. A show of kindness is even stronger than showing revenge. Kindness can conquer the worst enemy. It does not hurt the affected person, and it gives joy to one who has shown kindness.

People of all kinds and characteristics and mannerisms are held together by the golden thread of kindness. There is love smeared everywhere. Love without kindness is like a flower that has no scent. To prove that one's love is not mere pretence, there must also be kindness there. A society comes together and their heartbeats become one, when all the people around have similar kind thoughts and feelings.

Love has many faces. A mother's feelings for her son, and a wife's feelings for her husband are forms of love in different ways. In man's relationships, there are many connotations of love. But kindness has only one face, a gentle one, that shows peace and compassion.

Kindness can be read openly on a kind person's face. Conversation is in the form of silence. Even a hearing challenged person can hear it. Expressions, not sounds, make a kind person's language meaningful.

Kindness is not something that can be grabbed forcefully. It should be showered full of mercy on those who are deserve it. But it must not be begged for. Then it is not a heartfelt relationship, but only a form of help. Kindness is not something that can be thrust upon anyone either. Its value is lost if you give it to someone to impress upon them your own position. Such compulsory kindness does not invoke gratitude.

A gentle, pitiful touch is far more effective than a thousand such words. It can be in the form of a little assistance, or giving someone an opportunity, or even a mouthful of water. However ,surpassing all this is just a look, which will touch the heart.

One of the problems of our new world is lack of kindness. Lack of kindness causes wars. It is as if kindness and pity has dried up, and in its place anger rules.

Life's first lesson must be kindness, to study it, know it. Not ideology, but application is what gives it a place of respect. There are those people who transformed themselves from being full of vice, who did so not upon advice, but on experiencing kindness, which made them want to better themselves.

Kindness is unquestioning. It has only answers. The world waits with kindness.A mind that is full of goodness will understand that.

LAZINESS A VICE

Life is continuous activity. All living beings in some way or other are involved all the time in some form of action every moment. Some actions are conscious, some are unconscious. A person exercising, or breathing, working at his place of work, or opening and closing his eyelids are examples of constant activity.

Every being works according to its needs. Life itself is their work. Man has conquered time and space. The change of seasons has been to an extent controlled to suit his convenience using man's brain power. Because they lack this, birds from cold countries migrate and flock closer to the equator. Man how ever has found his way out, finding it comfortable to wear woollen clothes, or make a bonfire to keep him warm. Fish swim away long distances to keep themselves safe from summer or winter currents in the ocean.

Man who has been able to control nature, and has the freedom to control time to a certain degree. However, birds and beasts do not have that kind of freedom. Because of the changes man has made in the natural movement of time, birds and beasts find it difficult to survive. Sunset is when birds go back to their nests. Early morning is their wakeup call to set out to find their food. Mankind who has been able to bring time under his control, made a lot of time   for conveniently doing nothing.

The result of a deed can be good or bad. Sometimes even sinful. Then the reason for its defeat can be a lesson to be learnt for its victory later. A lazy person will never be able to achieve the quality of virtue. Laziness is an indication of weakness. Being lazy destroys strength of mind, and will take a person to a state of permanent hopelessness.

There is no connection between the state of one's health and being lazy and not wanting to do any form of work. There are those people who have problems with their health. In spite of this, with strength of mind they try to do whatever they can and feel they have to do, and also try to draw others into doing their bit of work and stay active. They know that laziness is the stepmother of all that bad or evil. For one who has done nothing all his life, but spent his days being lazy and inactive, at the end of his life he will have to resort to begging. Unfortunately, nowadays begging is a big job in itself!

It is common for a lazy person to postpone the task he has to do today, to tomorrow. The result of such postponement is that it will most often finally never get done. Postponing a task is never successful. Something nice that has to be done today, must be done today itself. One must be bold enough to and strong enough to avoid this bad habit of putting things off or postponing to another day what can be done right away.

While welcoming ideas and individuals we must consider also how they will feel about it. Just as we must stay away from those who are lazy and indolent, we must be careful to not conceive notions that may be impure or negative. The end result of wron ideas is laziness. The world will accept only that which is pure of thought and deed.

Contempt for such people will only increase their   dullness and lazy behaviour. When this lazy state of affairs comes to an end, then all wrong or wicked deeds will also come to a stop. The devil puts to test all men. And avoids lazy people! Even the devil is afraid of lazy or wicked ways! Society shuns him whom neither God nor the devil wants. This is the beginning of a lazy person's tragedy.

LIFE IS A MESSAGE

"My life is my message" is what Mahatma Gandhi said. Even today, all those who talk about life and its ideals quote this. Leading a good life rises above one of authority, or scholarship or being rich. An explanation of a good life would be in the light of the likes and dislikes of a person, and his personal and particular interests. The radiance of a lamp differs in different hands, shining brightly in some, or only a flicker in other hands. This is because of the point of view and opinions on life of different individuals. Even though everyone is given the same light, it is how one sees with one's own eyes that matters, one's own point of view.

Life is give and take. However, those who think of life in terms of giving are few. Those who believe life is all taking are the ones who push their way through with open hands to take whatever possible. To grab hold of authority is their main aim. If they are unable to get what they expect, they become angry and frustrated. They begin to think their life is full of misery and grief. Even under such adverse circumstances, there are opportunities to make life meaningful.

Life is is a form of work. When you are planning a project and you are working on it, if your mind set is such that you want it to be of use to not only to you but others also, then your life becomes meaningful, and joyful. 'Lives of great men all remind us, that we can make our lives sublime' said the poet.

The best moments of a person's life are those which he has kept aside for the sake of someone else, both mentally and physically. Ideas and thoughts need the services of the mind to perform. That is why the lofty thoughts of great people control not only their own minds, but those of society also, in the same manner. These thoughts carry on for generations.

The flow of time in life has been compartmentalized into yesterday, today and tomorrow. The period of time, when we feel trapped inside a monster, from where we cannot find an escape, is called the past.

Qualities like truth, non violence, kindness, love remain constant which is why we remember our great forefathers and their truths and sayings which we live by today. We remember their fight against evil, and their march away from the wicked ways of their enemies

Life is but a dream. Only such people who can balance opportunities and their inherent capabilities can be successful. When we are able to decide what we have to live by, we will know how to live to achieve our goal. This decision is what makes our present state joyous and peaceful.

Life is a journey. Even if the path to the future is not so good, we must still make the journey. Here is where our past experiences and advice received help. It may not be possible to always make our lives happy. Think back. We can still live honourably. This in itself will make us happy.

LOVE, BUT DO NOT TRUST
THE ENEMY

The enemies that destroy an individual are within him. It is important to recognize them, and keep them away. Such people who are unable to do this, are those who find themselves in trouble. Lust, rage, greed, desire, competition are within oneself, and given an opportunity, will come out and cause self destruction. Anger is what makes one's behaviour uncontrollable. Being quick tempered is a sign of a lack of wisdom, and then jumping into situations and conclusions gets one into trouble .

During the days of monarchy ,spies were employed to know the goings on of the enemies. There were eight kinds of enemies, according to them. It is interesting to note how they considered a friend a foe or an enemy. Friends. Then the enemy's friend. Even if the friend does not behave like an enemy, he can turn into one any moment. It is because of many such instances, that a friend was considered an enemy. There is a saying that if there is a quarrel with a friend, he becomes the worst possible enemy.

There will be enemies in front of you, and behind you. There are some who will work against you behind your back. There is the enemy who is in hiding, enemy of the king of the kingdom next to the neighbouring one, friend of the one in hiding, the neighbouring enemy's friend. Not only with respect to a kingdom, but also individuals have such enemies around them. It is from experiences that the saying came about that the enemy's enemy is a friend.

Whether in a kingdom, or in the case of an individual, there is usually a go between, who may not retaliate straight away, but at any moment can join the enemy's camp. There is also the kind of enemy who only has his own victory in mind. His weapons are defamation, baseless accusations, lies, backbiting and other such means. He who does not take any sides, so he is also considered an enemy.

In a family, there are four kinds of enemies. A father who has debts, a mother who is not of good character, a wife who is better looking than you, a wastrel of a son. They must also be treated as enemies.

Whatever kind of enemy he may be, treat him like a friend ,because he critisizes you more than a friend. Because of this,you are able to improve yourself. He reminds you of and teaches you things you had forgotten. The best gift you can give an enemy is love .But make sure you do not trust him too much either.

MONEY SLAVE AND MASTER

There is a saying that when money speaks, truth is silent. This indicates the power of money. We imagine that truth is God. Wealth can silence even God. Money gives both reward and joy. Life today is dependant on this.

Dharmashastra divides wealth into two parts. The wealth of God, and the wealth of man. The life after has two parts life of fore fathers, and life of wealth. Of these, manushadhanam or wealth of man is achieved by way of performing good deeds. Devadhanam or wealth of God is got by vedadyanam and yagam. One must perform only these two good deeds. Here money is not a thing, it is an idea.

Money is at the very bottom most layer of the deep sea. Pride and conscience and truth drown here. Status and wealth, need to be achieved in a respectable manner is the advice given. Experience has shown us that when wealth increases, man becomes a disgrace.

Wealth is not the be all and end all of life, it is a way. A wise person will not keep money close to his heart, he will only keep it in his hand. There is movable and immovable money. Those wise people who are always on the move, will not hoard money in any one place. Money should flow like a river. A miser's wealth attracts only ants, he neither uses it, nor does he allow anyone else the use of it.

Money is the life blood of a nation. The individual's wealth becomes the wealth of the country. Money does not belong to whosoever has it, it belongs to whoever experiences it. In order that everyone can also enjoy it, the government levies taxes.

Instead of going after one's own betterment and increasing own wealth, Vyasa in the Mahabharata has advised that wealth be shared. If money is hoarded, it will be destroyed by enemies, king, robbers or water.

All paths will always be kept open for money. This has been the state of affairs always. People who run after money are not respected, they have followers only because they have money. All this money however may not be enough to find a place in heaven.

Ancestral wealth, finding a treasure, profit ,fortune from a war, money from interest, agriculture, donation are the ways of generating money according to Manusmriti. Valmiki in the Ramayanam reminds us that to get money legally, use it correctly, to multiply it, and when multiplied distribute it, requires great effort.

Lack of money is at the root of all evil. Unscrupulous ways of multiplying money is the cause for disturbances in the society. That is why for a wealthy person it is more difficult to enter heaven than it is for a camel to enter through the eye of a needle.

A very big favour to others would be not to give them money, but to find out where their money is, and how they can put it to use. Money gets you enemies. When you advice someone on how to make money you will form a lifetime relationship.

MOVE WITH TIMES

We have heard that time and tide wait for no man. Time as we know is a constant, continuous flow. It allows limitless opportunities. When thoughts and actions get together they turn into opportunities which you must grasp with all your might, or else time will fly away.

Even as ideas of all sorts cross through your mind, time is passing by in front of you, when you arrive upon a new scheme, you also get into the moving mode.

It is normal for all people to move with the times. These people are generally progressive, but those who fall behind, are those who are laid back and who who do not have any particular ambitions, which is what they prefer and how they choose to be.

Most people just like to improve upon the lessons they have learnt from past experiences and do not wish for change.The leap into the future makes them extra enthusiastic in their belief that the older institutions must be preserved.

The students of yesterday, who studied in the the past, and who have understood the limitations and problems of those times, are the ones who now who think about how today should be.Their corrections are what cause change. For many, past experiences are improved upon,and with no particular inspirations, they just carry on.

We move forward today, improving upon yesterday's experiences. To suddenly try to change how life was earlier, and jump forward to new ways, will be difficult to accept. Only a revolution can bring abou such drastic changes.In order for quick social advancement, revolutionary methods have to be used, in the fields of government, arts, literature, science,financeand other ares. This is the philosophy of those advocating fast progression.

The three states of time are a creeping and crawling past,a slowly walking present, and a furiously running future.We are also thinking of the returns we get.

The greatness of the past lies in the good and virtuous things left behind. Only whatever is worthwhile and good lives on,transgressing time.Everything else is destroyed with the passage of time.This is called the division The good things and benefits that are left over, are required in the life of the present,which will be carried forward. However, thinking about what is now history, and is no longer practical or pertinent, to try to bring back customs is reality.

What we have today is good. To make it better is a revolutionary thought. Those who feel there must be change,will strive to achieve it in their field of activity. Although their hopes are pinned on the furue,they also try hard to make life today easier for all.

PATIENCE CONQUERS ALL

Patience is the special characteristic of a great mind. Very often waiting can be frustrating. Patience then becomes an obligation. Even when you are doing nothing, the very act of waiting itself seems as if you are doing something.

Sometimes a meeting does not happen at the appointed time, and one has to wait. If one is impatient and leaves the place, instead of waiting, whatever was required will not happen. Sometimes it happens there is a public distribution of a product. Then it means we have to necessarily wait to get whatever it is and we will get it only when our turn comes. There is no way one can push one's way ahead and get whatever it maybe.

Paitience requires a certain amount of control of the mind, to deal with matters slowly, rather the always be in a hurry. Impatience and haste go hand in hand and are willfull. It is therefore better not to have anything to do with them.

Patience is a beautiful quality. Patien people do not have thoughts of any unnecessary quarrels. Even in an adverse situation, out of which differences of opinion may arise, a patient man will have the equanimity of mind and the patience to recognize it and get through it successfully. The enemy will also then understand what a great virtue patience is. A person who is able to forgive and forget an enemy's actions, will find untold happiness and permanent peace. This is because our hearts and minds do not have place for bitterness. Love, gratitude, sympathy, patience are all siblings. All of them are always hand in hand and go together.

The foundation of all good deeds is patience. On the other hand, impatience leads to unpleasant happenings and their subsequent consequences. It is but natural to make mistakes, or for mistakes to happen., Both are human experiences. A person who can forgive is on a step to heaven, whereas one who has no forgiveness in him is on the brink of a disaster.

To be forgiving is the right of every individual, and a person who is able to forgive without being asked to do so, is an example of one who is highly cultured and large hearted. That is why one who can forgive is on par with one who is intelligent. An intelligent person always forgives.

There is a point of view that to forgive is a sign of weakness. This is not true, except that there can be a fall sometimes. Of course to forgive one who is not remorseful is useless. Under such circumstances, silence is the best remedy.

The words of one who is forgiving will always be sweet and gentle, to those who are listening, like enjoying music. Peace is the quality of forgiveness.

The mistakes of others can be forgiven, but when one's own mistakes cannot be forgotten or forgiven, it is only a remimder not to repeat the same.

PROCRASTINATION IS THE THIEF OF TIME

"Procrastination is the thief of time" so goes a saying. In short, whatever has to be done, needs to be done then and there,and not put off for later. The question of w hen arises in all matters. It is always good to do what has to be done right away. Unless circumstance are such that a postponement is absolutely necessary.

When we do something, related to someone or other, it is imperative that the person concerned is kept satisfied. On the other hand ,if what we are doing is for own selves, then the pros and cons of doing it right away or postponing it for later must be considered. Even if the financial situation looks promising at that point ,it is better to consider all aspects pertaining to it before you consider a postponement.

Planning and thoughts about what to do is what we think about when it is on an official level. It may be a single person, or a group of people. It may also be in chain form, headed by the managing director at the head down to the lowest person in the link, with different aspects dealt with at different levels and changes of plans .Instructions maybe from one person to the other directly. It is good for the one who plans and the one who executes to share responsibilities. The possibilities of things working out in a desirable and better fashion are more this way. There is no presence of a third party.

There may be many thousands of people around who are directly or indirectly affected by what you are doing. But since they are not involved in any planning, there is no need to discuss them now.

Any governmental decision taken, by the time it reaches the village officer in the lowest rung, has to pass through so many offices. Even though the problem may be related only to the person next to you .In the Lok Sabha a law is passed by the representatives of the people including the MLA's. The village officer enforces this law. However, there is no direct communication between MLA and the village officer.

In this kind of a chain formed by links, where different people at various levels think about the same topic, there may be no sense of resposiblilty or sincerity in the execution of the subject in question. The slow progress of Government related problems on account of of such hindrances causes great inconveniences personally, socially, timewise and moneywise.

Time management is of utmost importance for accomplishing successfully individual or social matters. Finding enough time during the planning stages itself of any project and carrying out the work accordingly will help in successfully implementing it. This will also give peace of mind to all.

Forethought and a goal must be the basis of good planning, although necessary changes may have to be considered while the process is going on. This also has to be taken into account. So in case changes have to be made, a second plan of action also has to be kept ready. Extra time for natural disasters have also to be considered, and provision has to be made for such contingencies. This may need even more particular attention.

Sometimes basic information may be necessary before starting on a project. Then later, further investigation on the same subject may be required as it progresses.This could be because the initial requirement may not have been fully understood. All this causes delay, so forcibly more time has to be allocated.

When there are many matters to be taken care of, it is not possible to do everything at the same time. So it would be a good idea to compartmentalise what has to be done immediately, what can be done tomorrow, what can be put off for some more time, what will not be a problem even if not done. Of course it can happen that such things put off may suddenly have to be done right away.

The important thing is to be in command of time. Things will be easy if one can keep up with time which just flies! This has to be taken into account, and kept under control before starting something.

One, two, three, four is the order as we know. One three and four are considered for practical reasons. Then two which has been ignored or pushed aside weeps silently! Those people, who in spite of being extremely busy, are able to understand this, will at the earliest possible opportunity take two into account.

Those who practice punctuality and enjoy the benefits of this, have reason to be proud of themselves. This will reflect all around them, and bring closer others who are around too, who will also be necessarily forced to practice this discipline.

Let us take a look at the social aspects of punctuality. The relationship between agricultural and social planning is feudalism. Land is of utmost importance here. The rights to the land is with the one who rules the land, the Emperor or King. Then the landlords, the smaller landlords, the ordinary farmer, it comes down step by step in this manner. This is how the authority over the land changes hands. If on the basis of inherited property, it goes from fa ther to son. In India also this was the practice. Emperor, King,petty chietans, Zamindar (in North India),landlord was how it stood. In different regions these positions had different names.

Cultivation of the land is the main occupation. The responsibility of feeding the whole nation is that of the farmer on the lowest rung. Rain is what is required for agriculture. Or cold weather. There is no surety about nature's ways, so it is necessary to wait for rain to start sowing activities. This wait, the awareness of time, is a controlling factor in the feudal system.

The circumstances being such, it is not possible to be certain about the waiting period. Hence the change in the feudal lifestyle of sowing and other activities, over time came to be accepted. This is the same for India also. Lack of such awareness is a major reason for its decline in an agricultural country like India.

The abolishment of the feudal system giving way to capitalism is an important event in history. European countries colonised many countries in the world and governed there, including India. In India ,the local industries were forced to give way to imported merchandise. Many new factories were opened, and new products were introduced. Industrial revolution went further ahead than agricultural progress. Under the strength of capital investment, agriculture came under landlords.

Factories became the livelihood of people. In the factories, punctuality was of utmost importance. The time to arrive at the factory and start work was strictly followed. Because of this ,people learnt to be time conscious. In Europe, the industrial revolution turned everything upside down.

In India there was no change in the social set up. However, city life caused some changes. Factory workers and officers all learnt the importance of time management. The police were very strict about punctuality, so also the courts. One had to reach the courts on time. The law accepted no excuses.

Politicians who worked in public places, important people who worked in various fields, company executives, officials, difficulties of travel, and being unable to stick to time often caused disruptions in programmes. Sometimes there would be no connection between the time you were supposed to reach and the time actually reached. All needed to travel. Experience has shown that when a person has to go to various different functions on the same day, at different times, he is unable to be anywhere on time. Under such circumstances it would perhaps be a good idea to skip one programme which may not be of such great importance, and if you feel it will not cause trouble, and arrive at the next function which may be more important, and on time. This maybe more meaningful. At the same time, one must not disappoint the people waiting his presence.

It si very important at the first possible opportunity to make sure that you make it a point to attend the programme or place that you did not go to. There is a difference between not being present at a seminar, and not going to a general gathering of family and friends. A function organized by inviting the public, where the time, place and the subject matter have been previously decided has to be considered as more important .

Those who know the tricks of time management can survive lapses temporarily. But doing it always will give a bad impression. The biggest responsibility expected from a public figure is trust.The truthfulness shown in financial matters and the proper way accounts are handled is only a part of the trust factor If the chief guest is late, a person is late, even if it does not trouble one personally, it will still go against him. To the person who waits, his time is invaluable. Even for one who does nothing, his time is of value too.

Not now. This thought would not have been fixed in one's mind had a thought been given to the result of the procrastination.

Society is where we live in an interdependent manner. This goes beyond boundaries of states and countries. Financial and business matters and profit making are going, at an impossibly fast rate.It is important to realize the involvement of man right from the inception of a product, to its end result. A fall of any kind at any step causes much difficulties to all concerned. The world is bound in such a chain.

OVERCOME POSTPONEMENT

A constant refrain that is heard is lack of time. Everyone has a day of twenty four hours. Out of this a certain amount of time is put aside for one's personal needs, rest, food, sleep and socializing. One's own lazy ways and disinterest in work and boredom, and intervals takes away a lot of time. And yet there are those who are involved in very many activities and receive gains from them. Such people must be emulated.

Man is not a machine that once wound goes on and on. He is able to tackle big machines, down to tiny microscopes without any reluctance. Whether the machine is successful, or not is in the way it is put to use. How it should be put to use is also decided by man.

Man's intelligence and dexterity is to be seen in the planning and execution of every invention or machine. They will work according to need. The machine has no understanding or consciousness. Man, with his powers of understanding, controls the machine. Man also plans all functions and decides how everything should be. In spite of all this, to stay away saying there is no time is not correct. There is plenty of time in God's coffers.It just has to be made use of.

There are some jobs which need a certain amount of time, and this time has to be allocated no matter what. There can be no hurrying up the process. The flower becomes an unripe fruit before it ripens

. Nature dictates that till it ripens , ne has to just wait. To arrive at a particular place, be it by aeroplane, or by car, or if one is walking ,all need its own time .Whether by air, or on the road, reaching a specified place will depend on the quality of the vehicle. If the person is walking, the amount of time taken will depend on the age and health condition and habits of the one who walks.

Usually a particular job needs a certain amount of time. If you just decide your own time frame, and then not do it on time, but drag the process, that is what is called postponement. The reasons may be many, or sometimes none at all. God tells you to do what you have to now,but the devil whispers in your ears to to do it later!

When hesitation or doubting or questioning becomes a habit, it becomes an ailment. In all matters there must definitely be concerns .Raising questions and finding solutions are signs of a healthy mind. You must find the answers to your questions on your own .Or ask and find out. Then you can refer either to books or search the Internet. If you still cannot find an answer, better to be careful that you do not slide into lazy mode and get taken over by the devil! Do not be taken over by him! Keep him away!

Resuming a work which has been postponed for a later date always ends up in a loss of valuable time.

STUDY WHAT HAS TO BE DONE.

Before you start on a job of work, you need to be aware firstly how it has to be done, then theamount of time it will take to complete it, and also what will be the penalties that may be in order, where and how you will meet the persons concerned with the job, there will be hundreds of questions which will arise. Experience plays a large role, and proper answers will come .After these initial thoughts of the plan of action, doubts must end. Then it is a matter of putting into practice what you already know or have found out.

A doubt may crop up suddenly. This or that? Here or there? This person or someone else? But if we stand around and go on thinking, it will not work. First you have to find the basic answer to what you have to do. It is not proper not to have a basic idea and then be full of doubts. Then nothing will happen.

It is not right to work on suppositions, without some basic

knowledge and some answers to what you want done. Unecessary time is wasted when you spend time looking for answers in the dark. The questions which arise must be relevant, and you must have a minimum knowledge of the subject Coming to a conclusion, and making a right decision takes up more time than what has been allotted.

Patience and experience helps in arriving at a decision. It is good to take your time and arrive at a firm conclusion, rather than rush into finding answers which may be wrong. This happens quite often.

What does the study of a subject entail and how to go about it? Once you decide to start a venture, and have decided what it should be, then the first thing to find out is how to find the finances. Then come the place, productivity, employees, marketing, profits.

The very thought of starting a business of any kind can be brought about by any of the factors discussed above. You may have a piece of land. What can you I do there, how can I put it to use.such thoughts will arise in your mind. Or you may have a good marketing network. How can you make it work for you? Or it may happen you are temporarily jobless. How can you put your skills to use? Such circumstances make you think you can do something productive. Out of this will arise the need to start your study. Once the research for your idea starts, you will begin to accept the changes all this wiil cause.

Research and study of the thought that has sprouted in your mind is essential, and will help in the success of its progress. You must also remember profits are not the only aim. Some social leanings must also be there. However, that does not mean you must in anyway be at a loss. Satisfaction and success in your venture must also be there.

WHAT YOU HAVE THOUGHT ABOUT YOU MUST DO

Dreaming and thinking about your future is certainly needed. Takea look at a forest. All the trees are not the same. Some give us sweet products, some bitter, some are in bloom with colourful flowers, some spread exotic perfumes, some do not flower at all.

And yet the beauty of a forest is not diminished in any way. That is the way of the forest.

It is very rarely that we find a man's thoughts, actions and imaginations fruitful all the time. Yet he likes to dream about his future, and finds time to sit and imagine of things that may happen.Dreams cannot be held back, but worrisome thoughts and negative imaginations must definitely be pulled back.

When we are able to control our thoughts, we are also able to stop daydreaming .Whatever we see before us, we want to have .We start to weigh the pros and cons of it. Whatever we see ,we like to think we should have and then spend time thinking about it.

Not only what we see, we also like to listen to what goes on around us. If it is conversation we find something to contradict. Some, without thinking of time and place voice their opinions and make enemies. On a rare occasion, an interference may help make friends. Yet in order to make a good friend it is not a good idea to unnecessarily interfere in a stranger's matters without knowing their what their inclinations are. Just as you imbibe knowledge, it is also a good idea to clear your head of unnecessary thoughts. Always have a clean and open mind.

Another thing is to not repeatedly think about the same thing over and over again. It may be an event, or something you have witnessed, or something or it may be a perfume, or a touch or a taste, no matter what,do not just keep on thinking about it. Some time forgetting is a blessing. But some times a flash of the old memory will occur.However, this must be dispensed with in a flash. If you keep your mind free of unnecessary thoughts, then you can concentrate on relevant matters that have to be taken care of.

There are people who drive, listening to music, or carrying on a conversation. But their sight is set on the road ahead. Here although other organs are at work, they are not wholly involved. Their involvement is totally on their driving which they cannot ignore. Just because a magician rides a motorcycle blindfolded, an ordinary person must not try it.

Sometimes when you are performing one task,you stop it and move on to another task even temporarily. This happens because of a discrepancy in the planning. The last date to complete a job ,the advantages you have because of this, the pleasure of those who are involved, the nature of the work, all point to the the fact that everything has to planned before starting.

Too much work is a cause of not being able to complete many things on time. This answer is an old one. When you decide to do undertake a task the time that will be taken to complete it needs to be taken into account. A heavy work load is when you are carrying loads on your shoulders and head at the same time. You have to understand your limitations of physical fitness and time management. A person who cannot understand one's own capabilities, will always find the workload heavy, however small.

The importance of the work that has to be done has to be decided first. Be aware of the time to be taken to complete it. Keeping these two basic ideas in the forefront, decide on proceeding. Do not consider big or small, important or not, but proceed according to the p lan already made.

When a job of work is done and over with,a big burden has been offloaded. There is the feeling of satisfaction and joy. However, rest is not allowed! A person who works has to now be in the mode of thinking of his next project! There maybe many jobs. Out of this, there may be one picked out as per previous plan.Then you have to consider the time and place. And also the different factors concerning the job. Then there will be the consideration of which has to be given priority. In short, you have to be aware of the tiniest factor in order to be succsseful in your venture.

Single minded devotion to duty is a sure sign of success.

SIMPLICITY vs COMPLICATION.
Everything generally starts in a simple manner. Slowly they turn into complicated issues. The reasons may be many. Sometimes because what was done was wrongly executed, or the work was done carelessly or various other reasons. What we have to learn is keep simple things simple, and not unnecessarily complicate them.

A person who does the same work repeatedly, becomes an expert at his work. This has become the norm in industrial places ,to encourage the same person to do the same work, This also means that the worker develops a sixth sense, and can immediately spot his mistake and rectify it.

There are many ways in which to ensure that our work load is simplified for us. One way is to make sure things are rectified and fixed then and there. For example, on a weavers loom, if one thread breaks off, the work will go on. But the quality of the material will decline. This was a small matter which could have been fixed right away in a simple manner, but was not done. This caused a series of complications, starting from the weaver's loom, to the merchant who came to purchase it for his business. The unsold stocks caused not only financial losses but also trust.

It is easy to make a simple matter highly complicated. It is always wise to nip the problem in the bud. Once it grows into a tree, it cannot be removed. For successful progress of all things, it would be wise to remember this saying.

OBSTRUCTIONS AND GRIEVANCES.

Sometimes there may be obstructions in the way of the work we are trying to do. The reasons for this are usually unpredictable. It need not necessarily be a problem caused either by the person doing the work, or the person getting the work done. If it is something brought about by an outside source, it can be cleared immediately. However sometimes the problem multiplies and then it becomes very difficult to correct it.

The obstuctions that come in the way could be due to various reasons. They may caused by one's ownself, sometimes it may have nothing to do with you at all. Sometimes nature may play a role in coming the way, or or there may be some social reasons. There must be enough time allotted to resolve such obstructions.

There are a group of people who are specialists in causing hindrances, and will shadow you as you go about your work. If it is an outsider, you can make them understand the reasons and carry on with your work. There are some, who in spite of knowing there has been an obstruction in the work, will come to complain. There are others who will tell you it is important to listen to the complaints, rather than try to correct the mistakes and carry on.

When disruptions and greivances come together there is a general lack of enthusiasm and interest in the work to be done. This again causes delay. The only way to avoid this delay is by resolving whatever issues there are immediediately. It is important to see that there is nothing in the way of the work, so that there will then be no complaints.

There is nothing in the world that can be solved absolutely perfectly. But we can try our best to find that perfection. This may be related to the work concerned, and it will be a relief to know it will end in the kind of perfection we are looking for.

Imperfection will not be accepted anywhere. The opposition, comprising of the complainers have made it their prime business to find fault with the work done, or the result achieved. If there is any job of work that is unfinished, rather than postpone it, is better to complete it. This is the best way to pacify those who criticize and complain. This is what will show the way to perfection.

THE FRUITS OF LABOUR

A person's physical and mental state of activity is referred to as labour. The word duty has very expansive implications like work, discipline, procedure, endevour, responsibility, occupation, observance of religious rights, ceremony, job, fate, rites following death.

The greatness of labour has been propogated in many different ways. The residence of a person who labours hard will be one full of prosperity. Even when poverty is wandering all around, it will not enter the home of one who works. Sometimes it just may so happen it will take a peak into the house and run away. There are people who consider spreading the advantages of labour, almost like spreading the word of God.

When someone raises his hand to toil, it is like sending up a prayer from the heart. All prayers need not be answered. But a prayer along with labour will surely be answered.

The wealth of a nation lies in its readiness to work hard, and in its intention to be victorious in the world. The result of this will be the reward for the country. The invention of scientists, creativity of artists, new ideas and vision of thinkers are all the result of labour, which is ultimately for the good of its people.

Man has been ordered to labour on earth, This is what the world renowned poet Homer has said. The skills a man has in his hands, he has attain ed by continuous ly and laboriously working with them. Life is a constant journey in search of food and knowledge and good fortune. Labour supports this quest. Acquiring knowledge and sharing it is for the progression of mankind.

Nothing can be gained without working towards it. We have heard about people having got what they wished for after long and hard penance. Silence and sitting still were also a form of labour, whereby they attained their wish. This points out the different forms labour can take.

Physical labour is the best cure for mental stress. As we move on in life, labour becomes more interesting. Swami Vivekanada has advised that we must be the master of our labour, and not becomea slave to it.

Whatever task we undertake, we must do it considering it our own work, not for anyone else. Only then a positive energy will flow into what we are doing. When we are working for someone else,it is usual for us to keep thinking about our remuneration. No matter how much we are given, there is always dissatisfaction, which takes away the joy of the work.

No matter how fertile the soil maybe, unless it is properly cultivated, there will be no satisfactory yield. Where there is no toil, in such a soil only thorns and weeds will grow. This is the way of a lazy life also. Unsavoury thoughts will enter the mind, leading to wicked actions. Just as an object left lying around becomes rusty, an inactive mind loses its strength and sense of purpose and becomes dull and weak. The mind is capable of conquering the ,given the opportunity to do so For this ,hard labour is the best answer.

Labour has dignity ,it is those who do nothing who are looked own upon. There are people who are involved in active labour ,and those who sit back and enjoy the fruit of the other person's labour. It is the hard working active labourer, who feeds the world, who earns respect and thanks.

The thought that springs up in the mind of every hard working person is what should we do next, not what have we done so far. While the world sleeps, there are those who are toiling body and mind for them. They have set targets they themselves are unaware of.

Performimg your duty is your responsibility. Do not consider or think of the result of this. We are reminded over and over again of this, about the reality and necesscity of hard labour.

THE RADIANCE OF RESPECTABILITY

To be a respected individual is what every person wishes. Although it sounds a difficult proposition, in reality it is very simple. However, the person concerned must put his mind to it, and go all out for it.

A person who is large hearted, who has an open mind, whose words contain truth, whose work is clean, and behaviour is affectionate is welcomed and has entry everywhere. The honour and love showered on them by the peoplewho decides their respectability. A person is considered large hearted if he is able to get along with everyone, and understand problems and find solutions for them very quickly .They consider the world a beautiful garden, If they are hurt by a thorn, they only think of the thorn as something provided by nature to protect the flower and perfectly natural. In all matters they have this positive attitude. They do not see anything that is besmirched, and because of this they have no kind of contradictions in their thoughts or actions. They forgive the other person's mistakes, and beg pardon for their own. They try hard not to commit any mistakes.

An open minded person has no secrets. He does not have to go through the tensions of keeping secrets either. He can interact with others with the same attention, keeping his own precision and attention intact. Even though he has his own opinions, he is not obstinate about them. His differences of opinion is presented with authority and a certain civility, which is how he earns the respect of others.

Mind, word and action are the three attributes whereby man interacts with others. The way to understand another person's thoughts is through words and deeds. Words must be truthful. Truth needs to be spoken only once. A lie can never become the truth. The description of a truthful person is not only in words, but also in deeds. Only then can he gain respectability.

Th e strength of one's deeds are dependant on purity of thoughts and words. It is the body that performs deeds or actions. For this purity of the body is also necessary .For purity of the body, there must be purity of the home. All these are inter related. Complete purity in all respects is the first indication of a respectable person.

One must be able not to hurt another's feelings, and behave with them without limitations. A person earns respect when he behaves in the same manner with all, regardless of whether he is a friend or relative, or one who has done him a favour or not, and regards and loves all.

Studying and gaining knowledge., showing bravery, trying to earn a place of leadership in society, none of these make a respectable individual. These are focused on publicity, in order to be known in society.

When the spring of goodness arrives, culture blossoms. Respectability has the fragrance of culture. It spreads its radiance everywhere, like the rays of the sun. Along with its own lustre, it lights up the world.

THERE IS NO SUCH THING AS DEFEAT

Defeat is considered to be the opposite of victory. However in the ultimate analysis of things there is no experience called defeat. Defeat should be considered only as a stepping stone to victory.

There are some people who take their actions very seriously, almost to the extent of intoxication. It is in front of such a person that defeat faces defeat. This is because his experiences may be considered as paths to his victories.

Victory has been the downfall of many people. In others, a small defeat has subsequently been a victory. Small mistakes have made them more careful. Just as right and wrong are recognizable in victory, they can also be recognized in defeat.

Sometimes the gap between victory and defeat seem very wide.At other times this distance is only as fine as the sides of a petal,so close they can hardly be distinguished.

Life's experiences create defeat which then becomes difficult to handle. The foundation of this is when expectations are not met with success. Misunderstandings and wrong calculations are also causes for defeat.

When a task is left imperfect,not done to perfection,this also is a cause for failure.Many victories come with the sting of much suffering and experiences of defeat.

Very often failures in one's childhood has proved to be useful in later life. However such failures in youth has led to victories which are accepted but not quite perfect. This is because in a young person's dictionary the word failure or defeat does not hold good.After a complete victory, there is place for not such a complete one, or it is an incomplete victory. No place for failure or defeat.

Being a complete failure is sometimes considered to be a good thing.That is why rather than do nothing, trying and failing is better.One who does nothing does not fail, nor does he know success.

Satisfaction is the dividing line between victory and defeat. If one is satisfied with what he has, he is able to consider and accept any situation as a victory.Dissatisfaction is what allows failures to grow like a tree. A satisfied attitude is able to accept any situation as a form of success. Such a person will not have in his vocabulary words like not enough, not complete, try again and again. He will have a feeling of enough within him, and a joyous look on his face.

One way to overcome failure is to have a positive attitude and a will to be successful. Believe that defeat is only an incomplete form of success.Then there is no need to be fearful. There is no need to look at defeat or failure like a coward, but face it honourably.

Before you judge the outcome of whatever your action has been, think of the situation you are in.. Then very often it could be that what was considered a failure ,is actually a victory. Try to be satisfied with whatever it may be and whatever you have achieved.It is when you try to change your self, and be someone else ,and when you compare your situation wi th another person, you feel the differences and think you are a failure.

UNKNOWN WAYS OF INTELLIGENCE

What is intelligence ? This is a tough question to tackle.

Knowledge is not intelligence, nor is wisdom. Knowledge can be attained. With the help of the five senses, it is possible to analyse and separate such information as we want, which is acceptable to the brain. And yet, the brain is not intelligent either. The brain is a storehouse of intelligence up to a point only. Those whose brains do not function properly cannot behave in an intelligent manner.

Some people who are spiritually inclined, like to think that intelligence is God given. Others imagine that intelligent people are God fearing. And yet there are examples of intelligent persons who have no connection with God. Like God, intelligence is silent.

Sight, hearing, taste, smell, touch are the five senses. Such matters that are obtained through the senses are stored in the memory. Some of all this can be taken out from storage by oneself. However, not everything. But if any one of the five senses comes forward, then very soon a form, or a touch or a taste, or a voice or a smell will in a sudden rush bring forth a host of memories so far tucked away. Like this, an awareness of things and ideas comes back.

Wisdom is the reason for understanding. When anyone who has a fair amount of wisdom, is able to use it at a higher and better level, it becomes intelligence. Whenever required, to have right thoughts come up, and then putting these thoughts into active mode, is intelligence. A negative thought rocks the balance of the intelligent mind. Such responses perhaps are what drags the world into wars. According to Tiruvalluvar there is no ruler that is such a burden on the world as that of one with no intelligence.

It is of no use just to have intelligence. It must be put to good use, to do the right things at the right time. A small percentage of intelligent people do however miss out on performing some task on time, because the right thought came to them a little late, by which time it was already done and it was of no use. This was not owing to lack of intelligence, but a lack of awareness.

Sometimes there is a feeling that a person who is silent or inactive is one who lacks intelligence. But when it comes to light that it is some kind of defiance, then it is viewed differently. A n intelligent head is far stronger than a thousand hands. An intelligent person can put those hands to work, or stop them performing.

An intelligent mind is full of brightness, whereas a dull person sees everything as faded. It is the responsibility of the intelligent one to bring to light the lesser one. It is said the intelligent man's tongue is in his heart, because of the way he speaks from the heart.

It is not from his own experiences that one who is intelligent learns his lessons, but also from the falls of others. A hungry person is not intelligent. He who thinks he is intelligent, is the greatest of fools. Life is a always a celebration for one who is intelligent.

www.ingramcontent.com/pod-product-compliance
Lightning Source LLC
LaVergne TN
LVHW091133180726
843490LV00008B/2948